YEAR 4

# GRAMMAR AND PUNCTUATION

Victoria Hazell

Illustrated by
Janice Bowles

## About this book

This book is designed to review the essential Grammar and Punctuation skills required in Year 4.

Each unit begins with a brief **explanation** of a particular grammar or punctuation concept. This is followed by examples of how this concept is used in text **(We practise)**. Parents or carers are encouraged to read the explanation and the **We practise** section together with their child.

Practical exercises are then provided to give your child the opportunity to practise the concept **(You practise)**. These exercises reinforce the concept and check that your child understands it fully.

The two **tests** at the back of the book can be done once the book has been completed. These are designed to check that your child's punctuation and grammar skills are consolidated.

If further instruction is required, we recommend that this book be provided to your child's teacher for review. Then the parent or carer and the teacher can devise a plan to ensure all the basic concepts are fully understood and consolidated.

**Meet 'BOB' – Back Of the Book**

At the end of each unit, BOB reminds your child to go to the **Answer** section at the Back of the Book to check the answers.

Victoria Hazell

## Game Cards Instructions

### Antonyms and synonyms

Sort the words into six pairs of antonyms (opposites) and six pairs of synonyms (words that mean the same). Are they pairs because they are synonyms or antonyms?

## Australian Curriculum Year 4

**Text structure & organisation**

Recognise how quotation marks are used in texts to signal dialogue, titles and reported speech (ACELA1492)

**Expressing & developing ideas**

Understand how adverbials (adverbs and prepositional phrases) work in different ways to provide circumstantial details about an activity (ACELA1495)

Recognise homophones and know how to use context to identify correct spelling (ACELA1780)

# Contents & Checklist

# PUNCTUATION 1

| | | |
|---|---|---|
| **Capital letter** | **ABC** | To start a sentence and a proper noun. |
| **Full stop** | **.** | To end a sentence. |
| **Question mark** | **?** | To end a question. |
| **Exclamation mark** | **!** | To end an exclamation. |
| **Comma** | **,** | To show the reader when to pause, and to separate items in a list. |
| **Quotation marks** | **“ ”** | To show direct speech. |
| **Apostrophe of contraction** | **’** | To show where letters have been left out of a contraction. |

## We practise

**The punctuation marks are highlighted in this text.**

Serena needed to have her eyes checked, so her father took her to an eye specialist. The specialist called out Serena's name when it was her turn to go in. “Serena, Serena Jones?”

Serena and her father greeted the specialist, but he didn't answer them, he just gruffly asked them to take a seat.

“Please read the first second and third row of the chart,” he asked curtly. Serena did what she was asked. “A, E, Q, O, P, next line, U, T, M, B, S, next line E, D ...” But before she could finish the third row, the specialist said, “Don't waste my time young lady!”

Serena was puzzled. Then her father whispered in her ear, laughing, “They are not letters Serena, they are pictures of animals! I guess this proves you definitely need glasses!”

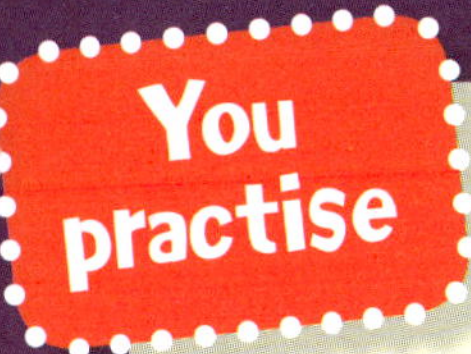


How many punctuation marks are there in this story? Record your results in the table below.

## How the Bear Lost His Tail

Fox decided to play a trick on Bear. He took Bear to a shallow part of the lake where he knew there would be no fish. Bear happily dug a fishing hole in the ice with his claws.

When Bear had finished, Fox said to him, "Why don't you drop your beautiful tail into the water, Bear? Then when a fish bites, pull your tail up as fast as you can."

Bear put his tail in the freezing cold water.

"While you wait," said Fox, "sit very still, and think about the fish you will catch for lunch with your tail."

"That's easy!" exclaimed Bear. "My tail can catch more fish than any other tail."

"I'll watch from the trees," said Fox, "so that I don't scare the fish."

A few hours later, Fox came back to the lake. The fishing hole had frozen over Bear's tail and Bear was asleep. He was covered in snow and snoring so loudly the ice was shaking.

When Fox stopped laughing, he quietly snuck up on Bear.

"Bear! Bear!" he shouted. "I can see a fish on your tail!"

Bear woke with a fright. He leapt up and his tail snapped right off!

| Capital letters | Full stops | Question marks | Exclamation marks | Commas | Quotation marks | Apostrophe of contraction |
|---|---|---|---|---|---|---|
| | | | | | | |

**BOB Time!**

# SENTENCE TYPES 1

**Sentence** A group of words that has meaning.
A sentence starts with a **capital letter** and ends with a **full stop**, **question mark** or **exclamation mark**.
A sentence has to have a **verb** and a **subject**.

The **girl ate** the red jelly.

subject verb

**There are four types of sentences:**

**Statement** A sentence that tells a fact or an idea, which can be true or false.

**Emotion** A sentence that expresses emotions or feelings, such as joy or anger.

**Command** A sentence that makes a command, or an order to do something.

**Exclamation** A sentence that shows **strong** feelings or emotions and ends with an **exclamation mark**.

**Let's see if we can find one of each sentence type in this text.**

We went to the zoo on Thursday. It was amazing! My favourite animals were the baby zebra and the pythons. It was sad when it was time to leave, as we did not have time to see the giraffes. We begged our teacher to let us to stay longer, but she answered firmly, "It's time to go. Please get on the bus." I hope I can go back to the zoo with my family soon.

| | |
|---|---|
| **Statement** | We went to the zoo on Thursday. |
| **Exclamation** | It was amazing! |
| **Emotion** | It was sad when it was time to leave, as we did not have time to see the giraffes. |
| **Command** | Please get on the bus. |

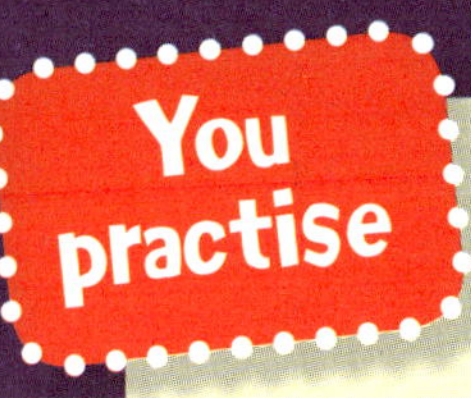


**Here is part of the story you read in Unit 1. Find one example of each sentence type in the story. Write each sentence below.**

## How the Bear Lost His Tail

Fox decided to play a trick on Bear. Fox took Bear to a shallow part of the lake where he knew there would be no fish. Bear happily dug a fishing hole in the ice with his claws.

When he had finished, Fox said to him, "Why don't you drop your beautiful tail into the water, Bear? Then when a fish bites, pull your tail up as fast as you can."

Bear put his tail in the freezing cold water.

"While you wait," said Fox, "sit very still, and think about the fish you will catch for lunch with your tail."

"That's easy!" exclaimed Bear. "My tail can catch more fish than any other tail."

"I'll watch from the trees," said Fox, "so that I don't scare the fish."

**Statement**

___

**Exclamation**

___

**Emotion**

___

**Command**

___

**BOB time!**

# NOUNS AND ADJECTIVES

**Common noun** A word that names something – a person, an animal, a place, a feeling, a thing or even an idea.

**Proper noun** A word that names a particular person or a special place or thing. A proper noun starts with a capital letter.

**Pronoun** A word that replaces a noun.

**Concrete noun** A noun that names people, places and things that you **can** see, touch, hear, taste or smell.

**Abstract noun** A noun that names emotions and ideas that you **cannot** see, touch, hear, taste or smell.

**Adjective** A word that describes a noun.

## We practise

Common nouns name the everyday things around us.

### Let's see if we can find one example of an adjective and each type of noun in this text.

**Did you know that ...?**

The wedge-tailed eagle is the fourth largest eagle in the world. It lives in all parts of Australia. It gets its name because it has a long, wedge-shaped tail. They eat rabbits, hares, wallabies and dead animals, and farmers say that they even kill sheep. The female lays its eggs high up in a tree on a bed of sticks.

| | | | |
|---|---|---|---|
| **Common noun** | eagle | **Proper noun** | Australia |
| **Pronoun** | they | **Concrete noun** | rabbits |
| **Abstract noun** | name | **Adjective** | largest |

## You practise

**Find one example of an adjective and each type of noun in the poem. Write the words you find in the spaces below.**

### Please Leave the Light On

Please leave the light on tonight, Mum.
It's not that I'm scared, you know.
It's just that I can't stop thinking
about that TV show.
The one where the witch came riding
out of the dark sky
and grabbed that girl from out of her bed
before she could blink an eye.
Then she took her away to a house in the bush
Where she lived with three cats
And shut her up in a little room
That was full of mean old rats.
So please leave the light on tonight, Mum.
It's not that I'm scared, you know.
It's just that I can't stop thinking
about that TV show.
And I don't know if she got away,
I was too scared to watch, you see.
For I suddenly thought that one of these nights
A witch might come looking for – ME!

*By Pat Edwards*

**Adjective** ______________________________

**Common noun** ______________________________

**Proper noun** ______________________________

**Pronoun** ______________________________

**Concrete noun** ______________________________

**Abstract noun** ______________________________

**BOB time!**

# VERBS AND ADVERBS

Adverbs tell us **how**, **when** and **where** things happen.

## Verb

A 'doing' word. A verb shows action.

The girl **jumped** out of a plane.
**jumped** = action = **verb**

The children **ate** too much cake.
**ate** = action = **verb**

## Adverb

A word that adds meaning to a verb or describes 'how' an action is done.

sang **badly**
the adverb **badly** describes the verb **sang**

arrive **late**
the adverb **late** describes the verb **arrive**

Adverbs usually end in **ly** or **ily**, for example, **proudly**, **lazily**, **bravely** and **noisily**.

**The verb is underlined and the adverb is circled in each sentence.** ***Hint: the adverb likes to sit next to the verb.***

He walked (quickly) to the shops.

I arrive (early) for school every day.

She waited (impatiently) for the doctor.

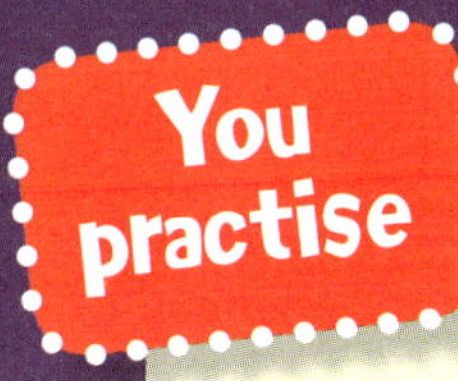

**Underline one verb and circle one adverb in each sentence. Remember, the adverb describes the verb.**

Harry easily lifted the weights.

We laughed loudly at the clown.

Mike carefully climbed the ladder.

She skilfully drew a beautiful flower.

Lucy confidently tied her own shoelaces.

You practise

**Use the adverbs from the box to complete each sentence.**

| annoyingly | carefully | soundly | correctly | gracefully |
|---|---|---|---|---|

I slept ____________________ after the late night.

A cricket chirped ____________________ outside my window.

The ballerina danced ____________________.

I rode my bike ____________________ along the edge of the river.

10 I ____________________ answered all the questions in the test.

BOB time!

UNIT 5

# VERBS AND TENSE

**Verb** A 'doing' word. A verb shows action.

**Tense** Tense means **time**. The tense of a verb shows the time, or when, an action happens.

An action can happen in the:

- present (now)
- past (an earlier time, such as yesterday)
- future (yet to happen)

For example, the verb **bake** can be shown in present, past or future tense:

| | |
|---|---|
| She **is baking** a cake. | **present** tense (now) |
| She **baked** a cake. | **past** tense (an earlier time) |
| She **will bake** a cake. | **future** tense (yet to happen) |

Verbs can tell us when things are happening.

We practise

**The verb in the correct tense is circled in each sentence.**

| | |
|---|---|
| The dinosaurs **roam**/(**roamed**) the Earth millions of years ago. | **past** tense |
| The dogs (**are eating**)/**ate** their dinner too quickly. | **present** tense |
| The canteen (**will sell**)/**sold** soup in winter. | **future** tense |

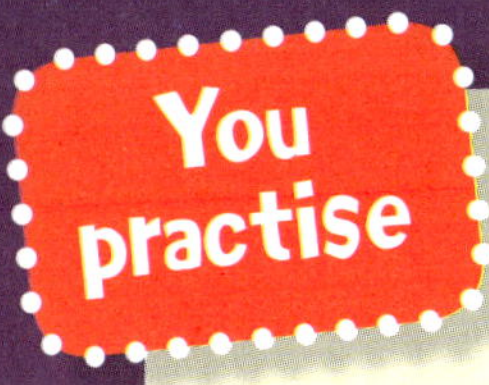

## Circle the verb in the correct tense for each sentence.

 1. I **am eating/will eat** fish for dinner. — Present

 2. I **rode/will ride** my bike to school. — Past

 3. She **waits/will wait** patiently in the queue. — Future

 4. They **will meet/met** us at the cafe. — Future

 5. My grandmother **sends/sent** me a gift every year. — Present

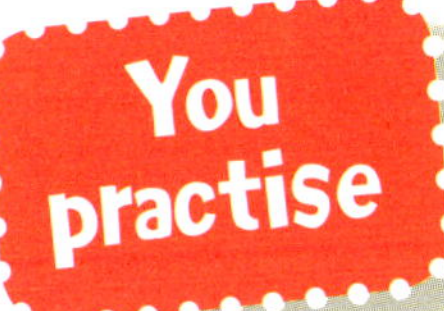


## Circle the verb in the correct tense for each sentence.

 6. The frog **jumped/jumps** from stone to stone. — Past

 7. The cat **walked/is walking** on the hot tin roof. — Present

 8. I **swim/swam** in the sea once a week. — Present

 9. She **told/is telling** a very funny story. — Past

 10. This **will be/is** a great party! — Future

# UNIT 6 SYNONYMS AND ANTONYMS

**Synonym**
= similar
**Antonym**
= opposite

## Synonym

A word that has a **similar** meaning to another word.

sad – unhappy

yelled – screamed

## Antonym

A word that has the **opposite** meaning to another word.

fast – slow

in – out

**Are these pairs of words synonyms or antonyms?**

We practise

| | | |
|---|---|---|
| sweet | sour | **antonym** |
| always | never | **antonym** |
| bold | daring | **synonym** |
| approval | disapproval | **antonym** |
| estimate | guess | **synonym** |
| gloomy | dim | **synonym** |

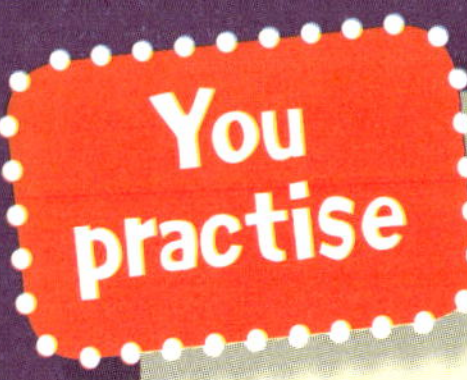


Write a synonym for each word.

| Word | Synonym |
|---|---|
| thin | |
| tiny | |
| easy | |
| break | |
| smelly | |

BOB time!

You practise

Write an antonym for each word.

| Word | Antonym |
|---|---|
| old | |
| sad | |
| long | |
| full | |
| boring | |

BOB time!

# PREFIXES AND SUFFIXES

**Prefix** A group of letters added to the **front** of a word to make a new word.

Often the prefix makes a word with the **opposite** meaning.

*re* + play = **re**play
*mis* + understand = **mis**understand
*bi* + monthly = **bi**monthly

**Suffix** A group of letters added to the **end** of a word to make a new word.

care + *ful* = care**ful**
thank + *less* = thank**less**
sad + *ly* = sad**ly**

**Prefix** = before
**Suffix** = after

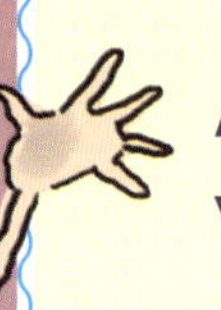

## A prefix has been added to each word to make a new word.

easy + prefix **un** = **un**easy

appear + prefix **dis** = **dis**appear

do + prefix **re** = **re**do

visible + prefix **in** = **in**visible

## A suffix has been added to each word to make a new word.

care + suffix **less** = care**less**

wonder + suffix **ful** = wonder**ful**

slow + suffix **ly** = slow**ly**

sing + suffix **er** = sing**er**

comfort + suffix **able** = comfort**able**

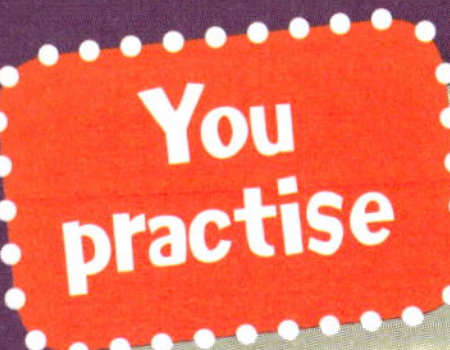


Use the prefixes in the box to make new words.

| un | dis | re | in | de |
|---|---|---|---|---|

 1 ______________ stoppable

 2 ______________ fill

 3 ______________ side

 4 ______________ activate

 5 ______________ respect

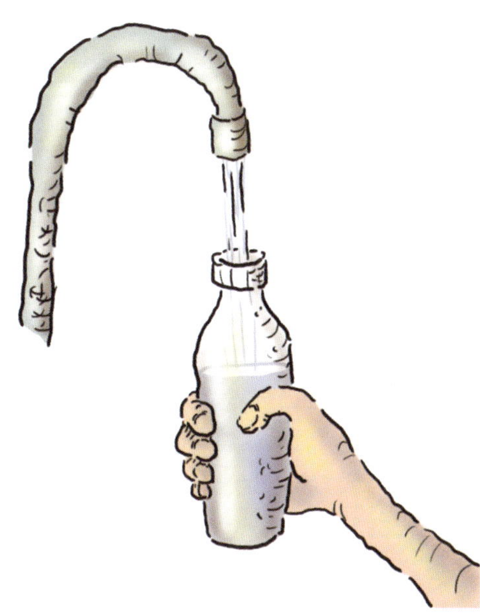

BOB time!

You practise

Use the suffixes in the box to make new words.

| less | ful | ly | able | er |
|---|---|---|---|---|

 6 break ______________

 7 help ______________

 8 cheer ______________

 9 sad ______________

 10 teach ______________

BOB time!

# CONTRACTIONS

## Contraction

A word that has been shortened, or made smaller. Contractions often make two words into one word.

Why? Contracting a word makes it possible to say and write words more easily and quickly.

We usually say **can't** instead of **cannot** because **can't** is easier and quicker to say and write than **cannot**.

Contractions save time!

## Apostrophe of contraction

A punctuation mark ( ' ) that shows where letters have been left out of a contraction.

**Here are some contractions, the words that have been contracted and the letters that have been left out.**

| Contraction | Words in full | Letters left out |
|---|---|---|
| I'm | I am | a |
| isn't | is not | o |
| he'd | he would | woul |
| she's | she is | i |
| we'll | we will | wi |

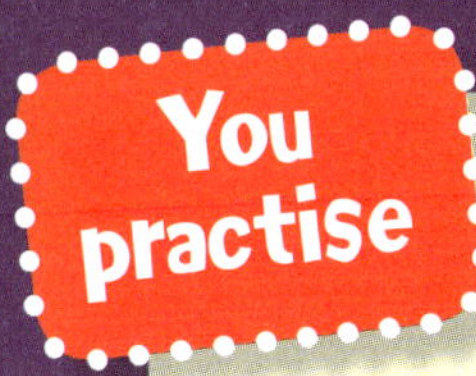


What words are contracted to make these contractions? What letters are left out?

| Contraction | Words in full | Letters left out |
|---|---|---|
| we're | | |
| don't | | |
| doesn't | | |
| could've | | |
| shouldn't | | |

BOB time!

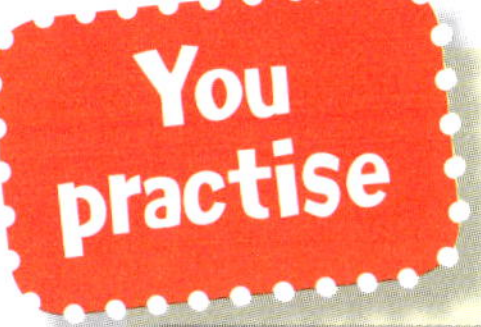


What are the contractions for these words? What letters are left out?

| Contraction | Words in full | Letters left out |
|---|---|---|
| | has not | |
| | I had | |
| | they will | |
| | would have | |
| | were not | |

BOB time!

# SUBJECT AND VERB AGREEMENT

## Clause

A group of words that has a **subject** and a **verb**.

The **girl kicks** the ball.

subject → girl; verb → kicks

When you write a clause it is important that the **subject** and the **verb** agree.
If the subject is **singular** (one), then the verb must be singular as well.

singular **verb** → kicks

The **girl kicks** the ball.

singular **subject** → girl

If the subject is **plural** (more than one), then the verb must be plural as well.

plural **verb** → kick

The **girls kick** the ball.

plural **subject** → girls

Confused? Read the sentence out loud and you will know what sounds right or wrong.

**The correct verb is circled so that the subject and verb agree.**

She **ride**/**(rides)** her bike wearing a helmet.

Caleb, Tran and Sophia **(walk)**/**walks** to school.

**The correct subject is circled so that the subject and verb agree.**

The **(dishes)**/**dish** in the sink are dirty.

The **(cat)**/**cats** is purring.

**We practise**

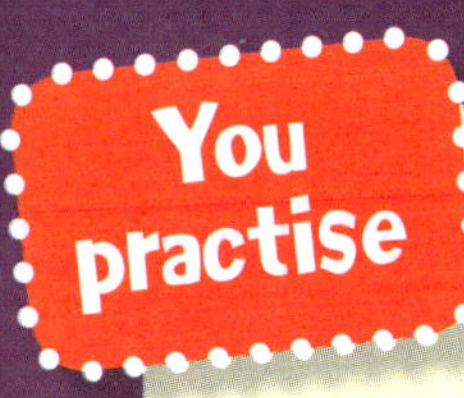


**Circle the correct verb so that the subject and verb agree.**

 I **am/are riding** my bike to school.

 Amy, Nicko and Sven **play/plays** on the same soccer team.

 The bananas **tastes/taste** great.

 The monkeys at the zoo **chatters/chatter** cheekily.

 My neighbour Frank **rock/rocks** at playing the drums.

**Circle the correct subject so that the subject and verb agree.**

 We celebrate when our footy **team/teams** wins.

 The **dancers/dancer** wears brightly coloured costumes.

 **Spectators/Spectator** line the streets to watch the parade.

 The **boys/boy** loves to eat popcorn at the movies.

 My **cousin/cousins** are bringing a salad for the barbecue.

BOB time!

# PARAGRAPHS

A paragraph is a group of sentences that are about the same topic.
A paragraph starts with a **topic sentence**. This sentence introduces the topic or idea that will be explored in the paragraph.

A topic sentence and a group of sentences put together make a complete **paragraph**.

## We practise

**These sentences put together make a complete paragraph.**

### Topic: Rabbits

**Topic sentence:** Rabbits are mammals.
They can see behind them without turning their heads.
Rabbits have 28 teeth, and they keep growing all the time.
They cannot vomit.
Rabbits can move their ears without moving their head.

### Topic: Rabbits

Rabbits are mammals. They can see behind them without turning their heads. Rabbits have 28 teeth, and they keep growing all the time. They cannot vomit. Rabbits can move their ears without moving their head.

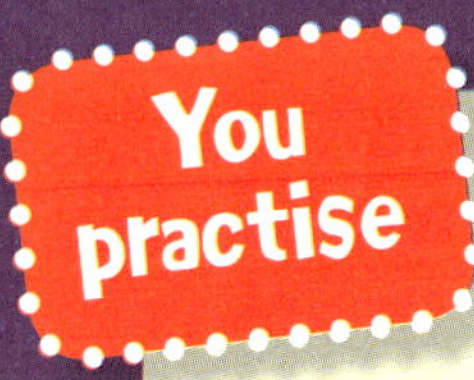

**Rewrite these sentences to make a complete paragraph.**

## Topic: Guinea Pigs

**Topic sentence:** Guinea pigs are very interesting animals.
Guinea pig means 'little sea pigs'.
Guinea pigs can live for nine years.
They have sharp teeth and can gnaw on anything!
In some parts of the world, guinea pigs are eaten as food.

BOB time!

**Rewrite these sentences to make a complete paragraph.**

## Topic: Clownfish

**Topic sentence:** Clownfish live in warm seawater among coral reefs.
The clownfish gets its name from its bright colours.
They are bright orange with three white vertical stripes and the fins have black edges.
The clownfish grows to be 5 to 13 centimetres long.

BOB time!

# QUOTATION MARKS

Quotation marks are punctuation marks that show direct speech (the actual words spoken by someone). Quotation marks are also known as speech marks and they look like this " ".

The **speaker** is shown before or after the quotation marks. The **punctuation** in the direct speech always goes **inside** the quotation marks.

**Quotation marks always come in pairs – " opens the quotation and " closes it.**

speaker — quotation marks — direct speech — quotation marks

**Mrs Hazell said, "Put your books away and go outside for lunch."**

capital letter — full stop

## We practise

**The correct punctuation for direct speech is highlighted in each sentence.**

"I love practising my punctuation and grammar skills," said Ben.

Martha said, "It was fun at school today."

"Do you want to go swimming?" Eliza asked. "Yes, I would love to," answered Tim.

"Excuse me!" said Richard. "Can you please move you car?"